How Therapists Dance

Poems and Essays

Dane Cervine

Praise for Dane Cervine's Poetry

Dane Cervine often lets a wry humor open the door to a deeper place. His light stroke sets the reader at ease, invites us into "the mischief in the young boy's fiddle," the "almost tangible, humming in the air between us" where, even through sadness and hardship "a blue dragonfly whirs" and we come to know we are "wide enough, finally, for every jagged thing." His finely-wrought poems are a comfort and a compass.

> —**Patrice Vecchione**, author of *Writing and the Spiritual Life* and a poetry collection, *The Knot Untied*

∞

While Dane Cervine's first book, *The Jeweled Net of Indra*, was woven with themes related to social justice and our larger connection with each other, this new book is flavored with the act of "attention" shared by the triune influences of his work: therapy, meditation, and poetry. Dane Cervine's poems are at once disciplined, sturdy, compassionate and wise. And there's an inspired playfulness, as in these lines from his poem "Enlightenment Is a Bitch":

> *...even fire hydrants with their red stubby arms become mandalas, and worse, the police siren revving its wail behind/my slow-moving car sounds like a mantra...*

> —**Robert Sward**, author of *New & Selected Poems, 1957-2012*

∞

Regarding the poem "Accordions & Shotguns," a finalist for the Wabash: The sheer volume of information in this poem is impressive—which is to say that all that story is fluently delivered to the reader—but it is really the passion and precision of the final stanza that earns my full attention.

> —**Tony Hoagland**

Everywhere I've ever been,
a poet had been there before me.

—Sigmund Freud

How Therapists Dance

Poems and Essays

Dane Cervine

Plain View Press
http://plainviewpress.net

3800 N. Lamar, Suite 730-260
Austin, TX 78756

ISBN: 978-1-935514-22-0
Library of Congress Control Number: 2013931522

Cover art: *Dance In Chinese Coat* by Marina Richterova © 2006
Born in 1962 in Moscow, illustrator and printmaker Marina Richter (Richterova) graduated from the Art and Craft College in Moscow, where she studied miniature, iconography, book culture and illustration. She has lived and worked in Prague since 1983. In 1990, Richter completed studies at the Academy of Arts, Architecture, and Design (Prague), specializing in illustration and graphic art.
http://www.galeriekrause.ch/richterova-marina.htm

Visit the author's web site at http://www.DaneCervine.typepad.com.

We Find Healing In Existing Reality
Plain View Press is a 36-year-old issue-based literary publishing house. Our books result from artistic collaboration between writers, artists, and editors. Over the years we have become a far-flung community of activists whose energies bring humanitarian enlightenment and hope to individuals and communities grappling with the major issues of our time—peace, justice, the environment, education and gender. This is a humane and highly creative group of people committed to art and social change. The poems, stories, essays, non-fiction explorations of major issues are significant evidence that despite the relentless violence of our time, there is hope and there is art to show the human face of it.

Acknowledgments

My thanks to the publications in which these poems have previously appeared: "Enlightenment Is A Bitch," "How Therapists Dance" and "Love At The Gun Runner" in *The SUN Magazine*; "The Gift" and "Enlightenment Is A Bitch" in *phren-Z*; "The Ukulele" in *Atlanta Review* (as a Finalist for the 2010 International Poetry Competition) and on-line in the *Santa Cruz Weekly*; "Accordions & Shotguns" in *phren-Z*, in *Sycamore Review* and as a Finalist for the Wabash Poetry Prize; "Imperfect Beauty" in *Caesura* (as Second Prize winner of the 2010 Caesura Poetry Contest); "The Taste of Light," "What It Means To Be A Hero" and "Prince of Disks" in *Red Wheelbarrow*; "The Fantastic Four," "Moving The Dark God's Hand," "Good Friday," "Naked," "Turning Fifty," "Signs" and "Sake & Satori" in *Porter Gulch Review*; "Sake & Satori" and "Camouflage" in the *Santa Cruz Comic News*; "The Secret Lives of Others" in *Poets &Artists*; "The Art of Therapy" and "Enlightenment Is A Bitch" in *Raleigh Review*; "The Golden Germ," "Chimera" and "The Visitation" in CONVERGENCE; "The Sound of One Angel Clapping (Falling)" in *Freshwater*; "Sin" in *Freshwater* and in the anthology *Harvest From the Emerald Orchard Anthology*; "Buddha Hanger" in *Porcupine*; "What Infinity Can Never Bring" in *Porcupine* and also published as a Bookshop Santa Cruz broadside for National Poetry Month; "The Meaning of Life" and "The Anonymity of Poets" in *NEBO* and in the anthology *Harvest From the Emerald Orchard Anthology*; "Fist, Palm, Hand" in CHEST *Pectoriloquy*, and in the anthology *When On The Mountain* from Holy Cow Press; "Which Way Is Heaven?" in *The Eloquent Atheist* and in the *Second Atheist Poetry Anthology* from Incarnate Muse Press; "Fame" in *Paper Street Press*; "May The Serpent Be Unbroken" in TOPOS: *A Journal of International Poetry*; "The Same Language" in *ROUX Magazine*; "The Magic Trick" in CONTE; "At The Entrance To The Santa Cruz Wharf" in *MiPoesias*; "Small Pebbles In The Heart," "In The Beginning" and "A New Science of Prayer" in *Ruminate*; "The Soles of My Feet are Borne Upon The Earth" in *Rock & Sling*; "The Chapel in the Heart's Bureaucracy" and "The Devil's Blues" in *Monterey Poetry Review*; "Adam Naming The Spring in Central Park" in *Cider Press Review*; "How To Know God" in *Buckle &* and in the anthology *Harvest From the Emerald Orchard*; "Why I Love Fundamentalists" in *Illya's Honey* and in *Sport Literate*; "After The Amputation" in *Birmingham Poetry Review*; "Leaning Towards The Southern Hemisphere" in *POETALK*; and "Grace" in *Red Wheelbarrow* under the title "Esalen." Many of the poems in this book appeared in earlier chapbooks published by the author as *One Pony Press* editions.

Contents

Chimera

Signs

The Art of Suffering

Foreword

Books of poetry often dispense with introductory comments. However, I would like to orient the reader to what you'll find in these pages, amid the cornucopia of modern poetries. The field is diverse, so pointing you in the direction I'm heading—a small map—may be of interest to some travelers. If not, fold the map into pocket and plunge in.

Here is *A Statement of Poetics* from former Poet Laureate Ted Kooser that reflects a bit of my own orientation. Ted wanted to be a writer, but flunked out of graduate school—so he took the first job offered, at a life insurance company, and worked there for 35 years. He said:

> *I believe that writers write for perceived communities, and that if you are a lifelong professor of English, it's quite likely that you will write poems that your colleagues would like; that is, poems that will engage that community. I worked every day with people who didn't read poetry, who hadn't read it since they were in high school, and I wanted to write for them too.* (Quote from the Writer's Almanac)

While I have been an occasional professor, love our rich literary community, and like Ted also write for fellow poets, still I offer these poems culled from the fabric of what has been mostly a non-literary life. As William Carlos Williams did, who wrote poems on the back of prescription pads as he went about his day as a practicing physician. My poetry has similarly emerged from the rhythms of daily work as a therapist and clinic director. Of course, it is the same mysterious Word we all love, regardless of literary predilection or background.

A few words now about the poems.

The poet Charles Wright was affectionately accused of writing poems that were a kind of "incessant praying," a taint my own work might bear. Beginning with "Enlightenment Is a Bitch," and ending with "The Art of Suffering," this collection of poems wanders through a landscape familiar, I imagine, to Carl Jung as well as Buddha, Rilke as well as Freud. Along the way are poems inhabited by my mother's ukulele, a meth-addict named Bullet, childhood superheroes all grown up, fallen cherry blossoms, a prisoner practicing yoga on his cell floor, ruminations on the worst sin, infinity, the meaning of life—and a large brass hand on a wooden bar-counter inviting passersby to arm-wrestle life itself, *knowing there is no winning this game, but it is sweet agony to try—to move the dark god's hand, to drink him under the table, to be the one left standing, the one still madly in love.*

How Therapists Dance follows on the heels of two previous books: *What A Father Dreams*, and *The Jeweled Net of Indra*. Each book aims at embracing a bit of Emerson's white fire, as well as Lorca's duende (the Spanish sensibility of dark pathos). The first book explores the light and darkness inherent in family, marriage, aging. The second is themed as a poetic response to the difficulties our interconnected world faces at the turn into the new century. *How Therapists Dance* makes yet another turn toward an inner life entwined with this broken, luminous world: a terrain occupied by writer, therapist, and mystic alike. My brain, and profession, encompasses this triune approach.

I think some, not all, of the poetry emerging from Santa Cruz, California's literary region embodies a certain heartfulness in the heartbreaking matter of being human. My own path as a writer has brought me to a triune intersection between therapy, meditation, and word—their shared secret involving an unflinching act of attention to the vicissitudes of the human condition. With heart. This approach is sometimes accused of naiveté by a post-modern world which prefers to approach emotion indirectly—and the heart does demand depth, complexity, in order to express its full range of tone. Perhaps a path through this tension is a poetry dipped in a bittersweet nostalgia that Edward Hirsch also finds in Fado and Brazilian music. He says,

> *Whereas we tend to consign a dark nostalgia to the all-encompassing category of sentimentality, thereby trivializing and dismissing it, the Hispanic sensibility has wisely saved it as a poignant and durable feeling related to the transitoriness of life. "Duende" and "saudade" are two Hispanic names for something we don't have an official word or term for in English, but can recognize when manifested in music and called back in poetry.*

My own writing has been influenced by this sensibility we have no name for—thanks, in part, to Robert Bly's marvelous introduction of so many Spanish poets into North American consciousness.

Amid poetry's modern landscape where a certain mental distance, according to Tony Hoagland, is often the distinctive feature—sometimes antithetical to Poetry's other enterprise, that of strong feeling—I offer these poems as an orienting toward Tony's "Poetries of Continuity,"* where narrative and language conspire to tell a human story, one open to meaning rather than dissociation. Or as Dean Young says, "Poetry atrophies when it strays too far from the human pang." Ultimately, of course, all poetry paints the many shades of what it is to be human.

Dane Cervine

Santa Cruz, California

*Note: See Tony Hoagland's excellent article entitled "Fear of Narrative and the Skittery Poem of Our Moment" in the March 2006 edition of POETRY.

Chimera

Even in Kyoto—
Hearing the cuckoo's cry—
I long for Kyoto.
—Basho

My love is infinite.
I could use a bigger jar.
—Len Anderson

Enlightenment Is a Bitch

At first it isn't so bad—a taste of ecstasy,
the world covered in honey. Even snails
scrawl the names of Buddhas with their silvery trails.

But then, too much. Pears become unbearable,
wet white flesh so tender one could perish
contemplating the first taste.

Meditation becomes oddly redundant,
attention now like water, absorbed in tree-root,
plumbing; even fire hydrants with their red

stubby arms become mandalas, and worse,
the police siren revving its wail behind
my slow-moving car sounds like a mantra.

Even my wife's complaints about me finally
sound true. I just bow. Kiss her slender hands.
Carry the garbage outside, but damn! The moon!

How Therapists Dance

Washington DC after a conference,
we head into the urban night
led by the jive-talking white ghetto boy
raised in black foster homes
bent on showing us the town. We
wander from night club to bar,
a mix of Black, Asian, Latino, White
earnest saviors eager to party, to strip
the mind of diagnostic prognostication,
to revel. Eventually, one by one, our group
slips back to the hotel till I am alone
with a young black woman who says
I want to show you one more place.
Down an alley, she leads me to a club
where I am the only white face in the joint,
and while she is gone to the bathroom,
the owner saunters over, asks how I'm doing,
says *if you have any trouble here, come find me.*
And I am suddenly more alone
than ever, till my young friend returns,
looks at my anxious face, smiles, says
this is what I wanted to show you.

Accordions & Shotguns

Opal stands with an accordion at twenty-one years of age,
on the steps of the family's 49th Street house in Los Angeles.
It is 1934, and the land of angels breathes in then out
like the ribs of her instrument. My father poses next,
little brother, all of six years old, shoeless, grinning,
the world spread out in front of him like an endless field
through which he runs. The back alleys and parks,
strewn with beaten trash can lid shields and stick swords,
Chinese boys behind the market tossing rocks like grenades,
the sand at Venice Beach where black kids would wrestle
with brown and the white of his skin didn't matter
because the city was his, he didn't need much,
was protected from harm, from the want there was by dashing older
brothers who'd appear as right out of a movie screen,
with their polished white shoes and slicked back Hollywood hair,
letting him reach deep into pocket to fish out fistfuls of coin,
who'd show up the very day the electricity was to be turned off,
lay a few grey-green bills in mother's calloused hands,
the ones that had been up all night wringing and folding
in hard-bitten prayer, the miracles that always seemed to follow:
a pair of shoes, a bag of groceries. A young boy,
he had no word for *depression*,

neither the 30's, nor his own that would come later.
There was no such thing as not enough, only the wonder
of what you had, the house where so many relatives came
and went, his bed a couch, this bevy of siblings,
lovers and wives old as uncles and aunts,
being the youngest of twelve, the tag-a-long,
and always the next miracle they brought.

Like shotguns in the desert, Opal and Lloyd and brother Leslie
out in the Mohave, cooking eggs and bacon at dawn,
cocking their huge, long rifles loaded with shells—
hunting rabbit, hunting what you can still find when you're young, and
your country's young, and the war is still a ways off,
and the world's a swirling dream you can shoot at
in the hugeness of sky and not worry
about a thing. Later,

those things would happen: accordion lost with its music;
shotguns emptied, buried in the basement; a war or two
working their way through onto Hollywood screen,
and you'd barely recognize anything—
what your life was to become, what it actually became,
the miracle that it is still somehow yours,
that you love it anyway—how you carry the violence
like a spent shell in your pocket to remember,
your ribs expanding and contracting
with each breath as though you are an instrument
life is still learning how to play.

The Ukulele

I was talking about family with Robert over lunch,
how I had traveled to Oklahoma to be the minister
at Aunt Opal's funeral, sing old hymns
like my family did in the Church of the Nazarene—
the six of us next to the pulpit while mom played
the ukulele, which she learned in Hawaii as a young teacher.
Robert, with his eye for keeping family alive in verse
said *you should put that in a poem*, the ukulele,
you know, how odd in a church, and this was the way
of my family, always a little odd but with a kind of music.
Four strings of siblings, my father the wood, my mother
the one strumming us into sound. I remember
swaying on the raised platform adjacent the pulpit,
my mother plucking the ukulele while we sang
they that wait upon the Lord shall renew their strength,
they shall mount up with wings as eagles which,
with a ukulele sounded almost heretical.
But this was our beauty: a string, a person, a chord,
a family twining the exotic, the novel,
into new tradition. Years later, making Opal
a family video, we gathered in the Japanese hexagon
my father built, singing the old hymn again
with mom's ukulele, but humorously,
dancing Mexican puppets punctuating
the air with raised fists as we sang,
our lives resonant with quirky joy.
This is what I was thinking,
looking at Robert over tea, the way family
endures, quivering as a plucked string—
the ukulele almost tangible, humming
in the air between us.

The Fantastic Four

After the phone call with my three siblings,
I remember our childhood, the four of us pretending
to be *The Fantastic Four* superheroes from Marvel comics:
Stretcho, the Invisible Girl, her brother the Torch,
their rock-man friend The Thing. Each imbued with a gift—
elasticity, invisibility, fire, strength. My two brothers,
my sister and I, perfect incarnations of this quartet
as we'd run the sidewalks confronting the hidden villains
of quiet suburban streets. Looming in the distance,
the adult world of parents sagging onto couches at day's end,
wistfully lingering over Ray Charles'
Take These Chains From My Heart and Set Me Free.
It was a world only the brave could face,
which we did, slowly transmogrifying
into the adult heroes we wanted to become.
As now: phone cradled, silent,
mother's stroke menacing our horizon,
but the telepathy still working,
the call springing us into action—
an invisible force-field to bind us, together,
in flame, the irreducible strength of stone,
the heart stretching, stretching.

What It Means To Be a Hero

As a boy, superheroes were essential
to my survival, for without
Superman's X-ray eyes,
who could see the truth
behind bleak walls? Without
the Hulk's naked brawn
one could only cower in the brain's
hidden hallways. But
I loved the mysterious Watcher,
neither foe nor friend,
but a powerful being
who *watched* human-kind
in our glory and travail,
who knew, it seemed,
we could neither be tamed
nor saved without destroying
something essential in us,
but who vowed to witness
as a kind of alien-Buddha.
I wondered, too, if I was a Watcher,
born in the body of a small boy,
sent to earth to determine
if human life was worth such
outrageous uncertainty.

Years later, turning fifty, I still feel
the tremendous weight of uncertainty,
reviewing my half-century,
feeling each heroic moment
hovering over a black hole,
the Omega point of acquiescence,
that yes, it should never have come
to only this. But

I remember, too, how it takes more
than witness, that Superman
in the face of kryptonite's green torpor
was far more heroic suddenly human
than when he was speeding as a bullet,
a locomotive, flying over tall buildings
dimpling the ground below. It was
how he'd sweat like any one of us,
how he'd crawl to stay alive, fingernails
scratching in the dirt.

The Secret Lives of Others

Your daughter calls from a Utah jail outside Flaming Gorge, so of course you go. Fly to the nearest airport, drive three hours in the remote dark till finally you arrive at a hotel made of long trailers with four small rooms each. You think, maybe, you are in a psycho-movie. But your daughter is a meth-addict, incarcerated for credit-card fraud, roaming the country with a friend named *Bullet*.

It is almost midnight. You consider the dirty trailers, ask to sleep instead in the jail because it's safer, but end up back in one of the dank, musty rooms. You call the next morning, but your daughter is no longer at the Flaming Gorge jail. The sheriff says she's been moved to Oklahoma to a federal penitentiary. You don't know what to do. No really, you don't know what to do. So you wait. Sip coffee in a Styrofoam cup, count the cigarette burns in the carpet. After awhile, the sheriff says *go home, you should just go.*

Back at home, the phone rings. Your daughter is on the other line saying she is safe now. Bullet is gone. She didn't know she was being moved, but now it's all okay. Your heart is in your heels, calloused, tough. But your eyes are leaking and your daughter hears the water in your voice and says not to worry, she'll be moved to California next summer so you can visit. You hang up the phone. You know this is a story that doesn't end. You circle the date on next year's calendar in red, glaring at you like a bull's eye, like a scab that won't heal.

The Art of Therapy

On the opposite wall in my office,
I contemplate three wooden panels
with muted mountain scenes from Japan.
Towering forested cliffs, a small house at the bottom,
two men in robes dwarfed by immensity,
lost in conversation amid cherry blossoms.

It is how I think of therapy,
traveling through immensities
lost in conversation, the dangers
of sudden cliffs, of becoming more lost,
of falling. Of failing

to run one hand then another
through the fallen cherry blossoms
littering the ground with beauty.

The Golden Germ

Sitting in the small window cupola,
I watch the lush red bougainvillea simmer
against the gray fog blanket behind, spread
my Sunday morning reading amid green & burgundy pillows:
a letter from prison, translations of the *Vedas & Upanishads*,
a copy of *Therapist* magazine. The phone rings,
a mentor offering praise for my poems, and suddenly
I feel as though God knows I exist, that she's
keeping an eye out. My prison pen-pal has sent drawings
for basic yoga postures he uses to instruct fellow inmates,
confesses loneliness since being moved to a new facility—
no more classes or groups in the yard, just solitary practice
in his cell. He's in for a lifetime, and I write back
to make sure he is not forgotten, that someone
is keeping an eye on him. In the *The Unknown God*,
the Vedas say *Desire entered the One in the beginning.*
As the Golden Germ he arose...May he not injure us...
And I think it is a good prayer, therapeutic,
this working out of desire's meaning, how
to survive it. Each in our own cell—
bars of marrow bone, stubborn walls of skin—
the ghost in the body that wanders beyond,
becomes the fog, the bougainvillea, the prisoner
who for a moment, belly to the ground, arches
his back concave like a boat open to the heavens,
floats on the cement floor as on a vast sea,
lingering in the silence, in the early morning hour,
content. Perhaps it is all one
long peeling away, layer upon layer
to the sweet, ravenous germ nosing blindly
within every breath—extravagant deity
moving golden inside every sin,
every wounded want.

Chimera

It begins in the public restroom at the parking garage,
a woman and man in the far stall, the sound of zippers, murmurs.
It continues as I waltz down the Pacific Garden Mall,
saxophone lilting with moon, a night light as New Orleans
when the side streets pour their slow syrup of patrons
onto Bourbon, something fierce in every pleasure, every need.
I saunter into a café, sip dark mulatto coffee, feel each vein
fill with religion, the dangerous kind, where for a moment
you swear the world almost makes sense, and you, harbinger,
filled with premonition, could walk out the door, spill the secret
everywhere. Then it's gone, and beyond the window I see
the sadness of parking meters lining the streets, how you pay
just to be here: bits of skin, confidence, falling into empty slots
for a little more time. Always,

this smudging of dark & light, how chocolate tastes better
when the coffee is bitter, how those with everything become
so lethargic, or ravenous for more—as though it were desirable
to be insatiable so that one could still long to be filled.
And so it goes,

the shifting chimeras in bar patron's eyes as I pass
Costa Brava's wide windows, the mischief in the young boy's fiddle as
finger & bow prance along string and fretless wood.
It never fades, like a badly behaved seductive siren
swaying her hips round the corner, and all I have to do
is follow, find out what waits down the muted dark
of alley: bit of jazz, red of lip, pleasures so stark
I'd swear there's a chance of coming out
the other end alive.

Sin

The worst part is failing to kiss the ground each morning.
Or the cold pot of resentment stirred and simmered
well into the evening. Everything else comes from this,
grows.

It wouldn't be so bad if such immense portions of good fortune
weren't squandered each hour, minutes the long dead
would ransom their lives to regain.

Even now, ripe apples lie rotting casually about the floor,
single bites taken from each—there is
no worm, no snake...

only this failure to praise.

What Infinity Can Never Bring

I love the old men
gathering at Beckman's Bakery,
the hobble in the step of one, the sad eyes of another—
the joy of company that brings them together over coffee,
bagels, regrets. Even now, their conversation still lingers
on children, grown, scattered: *my daughter's an alcoholic*
says one, *mine's unemployed* says another. But then,
in the next breath they are on to other loves,
simple passions—as only the old can do,
eyes ablaze with finitude's fire.

The Meaning of Life

He is young,
a college student with reddish brown hair—
glasses, pimples, nerdy—slummy olive green sweatshirt
with Santa Cruz skateboard logo, short pants.
The old Java House is almost empty when it happens,
the soundtrack of bad rappish-punk finally quiet,
the café still. He gets up from a table across the room,
saunters to the piano, lifts the keyboard cover,
sits down and says *I'm going to make something up*
to no one in particular. At first, some kind of quiet blues
or jazz, fingers wandering across the keys as lovers
down a midnight New Orleans backstreet, then
a swelling as though the sea was looking for a storm.
Black keys and white begin to swelter, the devil
itchin' to get in, but then rise as an airy flutter
light enough to make caramel and dark honey float.
I am so taken by this dark whimsy that my ears
cannot tell by the tasting whether the world
is bitter or sweet. In the listening, all the dogs
in me drop their bones, their incessant gnawing,
lie back and paw the air, soft underbellies
willing to be exposed, to be rubbed, to be taken.
And all the prosecutors in me cease their endless
bickering over life's purpose, whether it is, finally,
more good than bad, and couldn't it have been planned
a little better. Because here, in this music, this strange
improvisation, is the sound I have been looking for
all my life. A reconciliation of dark and light
in this tickle and tease of funny bone, this heat
in the groin, this flutter of heart as a hummingbird
pressing nectar into my raised mouth—all this
as though God were here, now, as this pimply faced prodigy
haunting the piano stool, improvising, lost in music,
shoulders hunched and swaying, giving it all away for free.

Fist, Palm, Hand

> *Your hand opens and closes and open and closes.*
> *If it were always a fist or always stretched open,*
> *you would be paralyzed.*   —Rumi

During my mother's stroke, her left arm swung
suddenly at her side like a stranger. She called out,
was rushed to the hospital by ambulance.
Now, recovering, her hand won't unfold—fingers curled,
supple, but unable to fist or extend. I think of this,
standing alone outside St. Agnes Hospital in Fresno at night
by the stone statue of Jesus, at the end of a spiral stone path,
my palms extended in prayer or defense under
the thousand blind eyes of heaven, sparkling. I make a fist,
then open each palm, then fist each hand again and again, remembering.

The next morning, I wake in the Red Roof Inn's pale room
next to the Korean Mart and the Jack in the Box—
the incessant air conditioner already battling the incessant heat.
I stare at a photo of my father, dead four years now,
but still speaking to me. His hand on his tool belt,
his heart full of fists, of waving palms,
the valves opening and closing, opening and closing, finally
closing. If he were always open, rather than mysterious,
even dark, I would never have questioned, never pushed
into the depths, would have been paralyzed by light.

Holding my mother's arm as we walk now to the car,
we pause by a fountain, a statue of two young girls running
to touch six birds escaping into flight, hear the sound
of falling water on blue tile. The stone girls
will never reach even one bird, but my mother,
already, begins to flex the fingers of her stricken hand
open, then closed, then open.

Imperfect Beauty

I think of my father while waiting
at the City Planning Department—
only one person in line, still it takes an hour
to finish this permit business. Details,
payment of fees, plan-checks for plumbing,
fire, electricity. He would have liked
this pamphlet entitled *Green Building Glossary*,
about flow-reducer fly ash, pressed earthen blocks,
straw bale, bamboo. The country is crowded,
he knew, every inch governed, cross-checked,
built to survive earthquake, hurricane, loss.
So he found his own patch of ground,
thirty-eight acres bordered by national forest.
I remember him waking sleepless nights
with a design in his dreams—hexagons—
which he built by inspiration, irregular,
marvelous. A small village, with rooms
scattered across the hill like mushrooms.
That winter when the inspector came,
eyed this assembly of queer huts,
no house in sight—he had no clue
what to do. But hand on red-tag form,
hesitating as snow began to fall,
my father winked, said *I'd sure hate*
for you to get snowed in here. Anxious,
the inspector closed his pad, nodded,
headed back down the hill never to return.
Years later, when my father too had gone,
I considered the efficacy of grief's
permissions, plans, the effort
to bolster sagging foundations,
rotted stairs. *If he had built better*
grief wonders, but what then?

All things end, there is no blueprint
for loss. But in the hexagon of my heart,
I still build his way—sturdy enough
for dream, for imperfect beauty.

Which Way Is Heaven?

At breakfast, my nine year-old son says there are perfect versions of things beyond earth, like a circle, like us. I ask if he learned this at school, but he replies, *no...I was just thinking about it.*

Like Plato, I say, *you've stumbled upon the world of Ideals*—and he nods, continues eating his cereal. The morning more perfect, here, than any conjured heaven.

Buddha Hanger

A rusted hanger abandoned,
melting into black asphalt under rain.
Beauty only the holy can see, and for a long moment,
I do—the oxidizing metal turning orange as a sun
lighting the horizon, a last goodbye.
Having held a warm coat, someone's favorite shirt—
or perhaps anonymous in a warehouse,
bearing a dress identical to thousands nearby,
waiting to be loaded, to find a home.
What more could anyone desire—
to be of such practical use,
to bear the beauty of others,
and when forgotten, to lie in the rain
content, letting go.

Moving the Dark God's Hand

Alone over breakfast at the Catalyst,
rain leaks from the sky-lit roof. I look up
from beaten wooden table to the underside
of a boat, bottom painted green, floating in the air.
Above, a huge gray elephant head looks out
through a forest of fern filling this old rock & roll venue
presided over by the Jesus statue lit with pink halo,
holding an electric guitar. Sometimes a haven,
however imperfect, is all you need. Reading

how Hindus don't seem flushed with guilt—
no dark concept of original sin, a fall—
I think *how lucky!* But turning the page,
there is the other side: so little passion
for making the world other than it is.
A conundrum: to be at peace anywhere,
or push like hell to make a heaven.

In the background, The Byrds sing:
> *To everything—turn, turn, turn—*
> *there is a season—turn, turn, turn—*
> *and a time for every purpose under heaven.*

At the wooden bar next to me, a huge brass hand,
fingers splayed upward, a challenge implied:
to grasp, to wrestle. I know

there is no winning this game, but it is sweet agony
to try—to move the dark god's hand, to drink him
under the table, to be the one left standing,
the one still madly in love.

Fame

I almost believe,
walking towards the exclusive
Squaw Creek Resort, that I am somebody
else. Eager hands assign guest badges
at this 49ers' Celebrity Ski Classic,
everyone roaming round the lobby like paparazzi,
looking to see who might be *someone*.
Rich middle-aged men eye with envy
the effortless, graceful muscle of football players
gliding by with leather bags—who return the worship
with youthful fervor, happy to be fawned over.
And the cheerleaders, short red skirts and tight white sweaters
framing bodies they are too young to know the cost of.
I am here as friend of the aging rock star
playing the benefit concert—my men's group his *posse*
for the weekend, and no-one can figure us out.
Are we members of the band, famous record producers?
Too familiar with the star to be roadies, huddled intently
over dinner talking of love, its loss, what it means
to grow older, to savor the life you have. We wander
the elegant resort, glide down perfect ski slopes
in brilliant sun, hang with the band before they play—
something about how normal we are creating an air
of mystery. After the concert,
another aging rock star who has donated
his flaming-red custom-made guitar for the benefit auction
calls up, says he's down in the bar with some cheerleaders
& whisky: but it's too much. We brood instead
over what it means to find yourself this late in life—
how if you could touch its worth,
you'd never sell your soul to anyone,
for anything, ever, again.

May the Serpent Be Unbroken

Deep in Costa Rica by a lush jungle stream
lives a woman who paints. She leads us into a room,
pulls an immense leather satchel from the closet, opens it—
sheaths of canvas thick with colored oils,
mostly of the black women of Limon,
large hands and bodies expressive because she could not speak
the language, could not say what she saw, could only show.
I ask how she arrived here:

white Quaker woman with bearded husband
who makes affordable bamboo housing that will one day
save the world. The acres next door,
planted with a hundred varieties of bamboo:
the one, thick as your arm that grows six inches
a day—you can sit, watch the world grow.
She says you just climb into a beaten VW van
before you know

where you are going, drive through Mexico,
Guatemala, Nicaragua before you know to worry,
land along a coast where old conquistador blood
mixes with indigenous, mixes again with black Caribbean—
and in the face of a world that doesn't know your name,
your language, your worth, you paint a life, a way of saving
yourself. Like the painting I buy,
composed while listening to a Cuban blues guitarist singing
May The *Serpent* Be Unbroken, rather than the *Circle*—
how the bright yellow snake appeared on her canvas,
wrapping round the clapping woman from Limon,
biting its own tail in a perfect oval.

Good Friday

After the funeral,
I wander the downtown streets,
my body a sieve: sounds, smells, sights
filtering through molecule by molecule,
and for these few moments we are one,
the world & I—fragrant smoke of cigarettes,
waft of old beer from the gutter—sweet & soulful,
nothing wasted, every detail imbibed
in this peculiar mix of cellular electricity & prayer,
the kind death seems to kindle. Funerals are the same—
irrevocable, haunting—my friend undone
by his mother's death, his shoulders slumped,
melting into mine, the immense cavity in his chest
that nothing fills. His eyes swimming,
as though he might drown, never find land.
I tell him

that grief is like this street: hammers & men
in hardhats behind cyclone fence, laboring
to build in the immense cavity a foundation,
to raise another human edifice on the broken pieces.
How we, too, rise from holes, from brokenness
again & again. But drifting into Hoffman's Bakery,

I think of resurrection too easily—
what if, finally, there are only endings,
and nothing in us rises? At the table adjacent
someone says the body is a mystery,
though it can be unraveled if you pay attention.
So I listen: hear the slow melancholy
of jazz trumpet in the background,
a kind of resonant, poised grief—think
   this is the sound of the world.

That without this somber trumpet
I'd be lost chasing light so bright I'd never
find the dark root of me again. That this
would be the greatest loss. For resurrection
has no meaning apart from blood, grief, cave:
how the heart—finally broken—opens.

Therapy

A television repairman says that most times a set is reported broken,
it is simply unplugged. I laugh, convinced my own brokenness
has darker origins, merits serious repair.

My therapist knows, pushing my buttons remotely,
watching me come alive, replay every wound.
The blank screen is in love with electricity,
the empty heart with its sad story.

At the Entrance to the Santa Cruz Wharf

Huge granite ball sculpture perfectly round,
with its twin cloven in quarters adjacent.
I run my hand over the smooth surface of the first,
gauging perfection—sit between the split pieces
of the other, somehow more familiar:
how we are opened, no matter the density,
the desire to remain whole, unaffected.
Then, running my hand over the pillared arch
nearby—fashioned like the number *Pi*—I feel
the endless decimals of my life stream out to sea:
an equation unresolved. I am nothing but metaphor
& bone wrapped in skin. How else to explain
the passing of days, the wonder, each gorgeous
uncertainty?

The Same Language

Dawn at Blooms Creek,
ears stirring while eyes remain shut,
sound enveloping in a way sight only distracts from.
Blue jay squawk, black bird caw,
woodpecker rapid-fire knock on wood
amid swell of feather in the jubilant first light.
In my human way, I can only anthropomorphize:
are they singing of sex, food, territory; gawking
at the brightly colored tents, the slow
cumbersome stirrings of the wingless below—
or is it a wordless prayer, immortal,
each morning the same?

Over tea, the fire warms,
aroma of lemon & cedar blending
with sight & touch into a single dialect of joy.
A robin lands in camp, struts triumphantly,
pecks under the redwood tree with bark
furry as buffalo hide. And the oak,
suede brown covered with green moss
elegant as scarves on an aging matron.

In the distances of the valley, the sounds
of children waking in other camp sites
stirring & chattering like the birds—
it is the same language, really,
of caw & bark & smoke—
the five senses a synesthesia,
a single unadulterated tongue
of the world.

Naked

My brother and I sit in the shadow
of curved granite walls tall as a two-story house,
the huge chamber open to sky, Cherry Creek rushing
over the highest lip down into a calamity of rock,
then pooling quiet and cold in this palace of stone.
We rest languid in the shade, naked after a swim,
sheltering from sun that has baked us all day
while roaming the endless turn and fall of river
through descending cliffs.

We are alone
in our wilderness of thoughts, in the body's privacy
until a blue dragonfly whirs into the chamber
skirting over water back and forth, lingering
while we begin, suddenly, to talk of our father
gone this past year, how he comes to us still
in the guise of hummingbirds, dragonflies—
how as sons we stand naked to grief
and love, the heart never finding bottom,
no matter how deep the pool,
how far the fall.

The Magic Trick

My father-in-law forgets, again, that his wallet
is in the cruise-ship bedroom safe, flustered
as he searches pants pockets for his identity.
Finally, my mother-in-law just gives it to him,
secrets another glass of Chablis, then another,
as though drinking were a hidden fountain—
memory unwrinkling into the young girl
she somewhere still is, though the body
silently cripples her cell by defiant cell.
The grandchildren remain blissful,
cavort across cruise ship decks
bound in their cavernous hearts
for what must seem an eternal voyage—
limitless food, incessant festivities,
the night shows. Now, all of us sit
expectant in the front row, the magician
pulling my wife from her seat onto the stage,
bra mysteriously pulled from blouse,
embarrassed laughter; then her brother,
dollar bill ripped in pieces, materializing again
whole, inside an orange; their father beaming,
his family whole, here, together, magic
his childhood hobby, hands clapping
as he watches the juggler in the darkened room,
fluorescent rings rotating three to each arm and leg
while hanging suspended from the ceiling,
teeth clenched on a leather strap,
an apple-shaped orb stuck in his mouth
like some original sin, as he holds on
for dear life, for all of us—the apple,
the teeth, the death-defying act.
That we live at all, this original
inexplicable trick.

Turning Fifty

There were omens as I traveled—
a one-armed man riding a green bike
down Main Street in my hometown.
Then again in Weed, a gray-haired man
carrying a monstrous yellow boa constrictor
wound round his neck and shoulders. It would be
this kind of year—stunning, sad—the body
compromised, but carrying danger lightly, extravagantly
as though aging were the most natural wonder
to parade in broad daylight, the strange manner
in which we become more and less of ourselves simultaneously,
no one batting an eye, merely nodding,
saying *well look at that*, hair, muscle, skin,
shifting, disappearing.

I know there is a young boy who never ages inside,
perplexed at how long a man's shirt-sleeves are,
shoes too huge to walk in, pants so large
I could hide in them like a tent. The same way
my mother, now seventy-five, says the mirror lies,
because she is no different than the school girl
dangling her legs from the bench in a world
where everyone is older than you, and your body
will live forever. But we are young, still,

in the spiritual sense of still being born,
caterpillars incubating in sacks that hum
with the transubstantiation of consciousness
of leg into wing, of doubt into color so varied
that even a one-armed man would whistle
pedaling down what remains of his only life,
and the gorgeous snake, wrinkling its fading skin
into useless husk, muscles its new translucent body
into another life, and another, and another.

Small Pebbles in the Heart

Picking my way round massive boulders along the river,
I see in the flank of one a perfect, small bowl carved concave
by millennium of rushing water, small rocks swirling round
and round as a patient potter carving in stone. Such patience.
Perhaps the mad rush of thoughts whirling round in me
—so many loose pebbles—will slowly, relentlessly carve
an empty bowl in the stone of my heart. Wide enough,
finally, for every jagged thing.

Camouflage

In the *Camouflage* store window,
blond wigs, red velvet undergarments, black lace
invite passersby to enter, become someone else—
while across the street a woman carries a red rose
brazenly in the light of day.
Bikers dressed head to toe in the blackest of leather
park their choppers neatly in a row,
while a beatnik with beret and goatee angles past
in a motorized wheelchair. If I didn't know better,

I'd say we're in hiding—
each face a mask, each body a festooned costume,
the charade a heart-exploding game. How else
to splinter pure light into innumerable shades,
shards of pigment, a spectrum of radiance,
the *We* that cracks into *you* and *me*, and here we are:
cut from the same fabric, holographic cousins,
this inscrutable camouflage our salvation
from the mantra of sameness, life the gauntlet
that defines the difference we become,
igniting the spark flickered into being
by the flint in the heart of the One.

And so the man with shaved head and cigarette
sizes me up, slowly drags the burning tobacco in,
lets it out his nostrils in plumes of smoke
like a brooding dragon, discerning
if we are of the same species, decoding
if I am enemy or brother, a long lost existential spy
camouflaged in the most convincing of covers,
or just another brainwashed devil, a lost angel
roaming life's labyrinth where no one gets out alive,
everyone, in the final hour, shedding this body

of lose skin—eight pounds of bone—
taking their 21 grams of spirit away.
Perhaps this is what the man in black slacks,
blue shirt, black eye-patch knows,
exiting the Vault Gallery bearing a fragile glass heart
for someone he loves. Or the young woman
in tight jeans, tawny skin, boyfriend tracing circles
on the small of her bare back. That the world
emerges fresh each second, a pigeon flashing
like a sword, slicing the air seamless.
Pouring warm through the song of the street musicians,
shining in the silver nose-ring of the tall blond lad,
the slicing bow of the Asian girl's fiddle,
her country song teasing *if you want to see heaven,*
Look! you're already here.

Signs

The trees reflected in the river are unconscious
of a spiritual world so near them. So are we.
—Nathaniel Hawthorne,
from The American Notebooks

But mostly I just stand in the dark field,
in the middle of the world, breathing...
If there's a temple, I haven't found it yet.
I simply go on drifting, in the heaven of the grass
and the weeds.
—Mary Oliver

Prince of Disks

Across the small wooden table between us
I spread the Tarot cards she has chosen randomly
from the pile, turn them over one by one. She reveals
her family lineage, many generations in Mariposa,
once proud, now poor: *my mother wasn't a drunk,*
just unlucky. Now it's her turn to be strong,
raising two children, waitressing at Miner's Inn,
saving tips to buy the broken-down house
she was raised in, caring for her boyfriend's son
with cerebral palsy. She is young—almost worldly,
almost angelic—and for a moment, turning over
the *Prince of Disks*, not looking as she removes her sweater
revealing an elegant collarbone, a hint of breast. I want
to marry her, to save her, some lost part of me. Instead,
we look at the prince's steel chariot drawn by his snorting bull,
rippling flanks obstinate, unflinching to pain, and I say
this is you, nothing can stop you, not the fatigue,
not the man who takes and never gives, not the endless hours
of serving eggs, beer—endless hours. Because this
is how strong she has to be. And when we are done,
her twenty-dollar bill laid on the table, her lips curve
into a smile, saying *Yes!*

Signs

Heading down 69 South past the Choctaw Nation,
on the way to Wilberton, Oklahoma
for Aunt Opal's funeral, I drive
through one small town after another
observing the signs of the times,
past *Paradise Donuts* and *Charlotte's Web Bar*
in Harlyville, each a small oasis
in the boarded up broken down block.
Fuel at *Lake Mystik Gas*, watch ecstatic boys
cavort in four-wheel drive dirt bikes
along naked dusty roads branching
into flat horizons eerily similar
from beginning to end. Driving on,

past the *East Branch Gun & Pawn*,
I see old trailers where part of America
lives, a flock of black crows, a cardboard sign
announcing *new peach smoothies* in a dark house
leaning right, then past an urgent black and white
message announcing *The Wages of Sin is Death,*
then *Halliburton* in black block letters,
and finally, a rickety wooden sign exhorting
Wake up America, God's Judgment is Coming.

Slapping my face to ward away sleep,
I keep an eye out for seraphim wing,
stare into the double-beamed headlight coloring
the coming dusk like whiskey.

The Soles of My Feet Are Borne Upon the Earth

Having turned fifty,
I trek to Gravely Ford in the Sierra mountains,
stoke a small orange flame with tinder
till it leaps, engulfs a fallen tree trunk
laid across a sturdy circle of stones.
The Big Dipper so low in the sky
it appears to be scooping earth
from the horizon. Last night,

before driving to the trailhead,
I slept in a hexagon my father built
in the woods, and in my dream,
a deer entered the kitchen through an open door.
In the morning, my mother woke me
saying Aunt Opal is dying in Oklahoma,
that the doctor recommends moving her
to a larger hospital to prolong her ninety-two years.
But we know that Opal—one good leg,
a mind already straying—has waited for years
to leave the body's insults, to join her husband.
So we tell the doctor *no, she wants to go,*
hear relief in his voice despite years of indoctrination
in medicine's stubborn refusal to let the body know
when it is ready. Now,

staring at the sky above the campfire's burgundy embers,
fifty years of memory weight me so low
that the soles of my feet are finally borne upon the earth,
closer than the heaven I have envied all my life—
its desperate beauty, its dark bowl of brilliant lights.

The Chapel in the Heart's Bureaucracy

At Asilomar, sand-swept Monterey pine retreat,
I enter the conference hall as I've done the past two mornings,
sit in my chair to hear a judge, or state official, or professor
discuss the despair of families, the toll of poverty,
the statistics of decay. By the second sip of coffee,
I notice that I recognize no one around me,
that the speaker is dressed in robes with a purple sash,
a black preacher just warming up his sermon—
the power of love, the way of sin—
and I sheepishly look at my program to locate
my own plenary. But really, I don't want to leave,

don't want to hear legislative analysts discuss
the latest school funding crisis, or suicide's stain,
or how prisons gobble up disaffected youth
as the only university we afford them.
I want to feel the word *sin* seep across every budget cut,
the word *love* lilt its way into the vocabulary
of every director, every politician, each voting citizen.

So when at last I find my own conference
in Asilomar's original chapel, hear a state director
say his own son was denied health insurance
because of depression, I wonder about the heart
of this country, if it is the wrong liturgy we chant—
one of policy and politics rather than love's bare sound.
Hear the bell ringing twelve tones in the chapel's steeple
as it ushers us out as secret missionaries
to a world weary of love's absence,
of sin's bureaucracy, a world waiting
as a lover once abandoned listens
for the door to open.

Adam Naming the Spring In Central Park

Along the lake, *turtles!*

Nearby, *American Robin, Eastern Phoebe*—
he can't remember, is it he who gives
the name, or does each name emerge
from the canopy as *Baltimore Oriole,*
as *Scarlet Tanager.*

Running his hand along the tree trunks, spying
Northern Flicker, White-breasted Nuthatch,
he rolls each syllable over tongue. Then,
lazing on the ground, pronounces *Hooded Warbler,*
Winter Wren as they sidle away.

After awhile (century, eon?) he bounds into water,
splashes *Mallard,* splashes *Double-crested Cormorant,*
floats on his back peering at sky rustled by
Peregrine Falcon, Ring-billed Gull, each wing
whispering hieroglyphic sound in his clay ear.

Climbing into sub-canopy, he coos *Wood thrush,*
Cedar Waxwing, stammers *Northern Mockingbird*
and *Brown Thrasher* as he chases among the shrubs,
till breathless, standing on the lake's shore again,
silently mouths *Great Egret, Spotted Sandpiper.*

And amid *Mica Schist, White Birch, Wisteria,*
his tongue flags, fails at the sight of turtles again
lined-up sunning on the large branch fallen in the lake.
The largest one of all, submerged, nosing the air,
crooked mouth uttering, he swears,
the silent syllable *God.*

A New Science of Prayer

We were curled by the fire, six of us ruminating
on lives still in mid-sentence. No one went to church,
most of us wandering into therapy, meditation, support groups
for anonymous wounds. The world loomed large—
a mysterious tabernacle—the jagged contour of war and want
long ago having eviscerated faith from each chest,
six red hearts pulsing under black sky as a kind of confession.
It had become clear no one would save us,

though the double-blind Russian studies
turned our conversation to prayer nonetheless,
how researchers mailed envelopes around the globe
to circles of prayer from every tradition—Muslim, Christian,
Buddhist—asked them to linger on each name,
savor it as a seed, a point of light growing inside the sick.
How the other lists lay guarded, idling on a researcher's clipboard:
no prayer, no song. The results,
while no miracle, spoke the language of science:
that numbers don't lie, that those murmured
on the lips of the faithful showed statistical improvement,
the kind any god would be jealous of.

The fire flickered in our eyes, six pair of rubies,
wondering what we'd fallen into these dark years
ensnared in our own sticky web,
a kind of martyrdom. Maybe we lived
blind to these strands of luminous reciprocity
that also connect us. When touched, rhythmical waves
arcing as magnetic currents through gray matter,
the miracle of bone, of nerve-ending, of muscle—
what we are, what we do, vibrating
uncontained by skin, swaying the world
one way, then another.

Sake & Satori

The debate went thus: *what difference between the two?*
said the street minstrel to the monk meditating
beside him at the sushi bar:
clear liquid or clear mind?
The latter, said the monk, wet enough to blend
the world's rough edges even after the cup is empty,
clear mind the language spoken at the border between *need* and *enough*,
cooling the sun's fire-branded desire beneath the ribcage
when the heart, burnt as the Djarum-butt surrendered on the sidewalk
is crushed by the boot of every meditating cowgirl or boy
who climbs back into life even when it's only
an old beaten Ford truck meandering down Main Street
towards the dusty horizon,
receding further mile after mile till it disappears
entirely—along with the driver.

I've a truer story, mumbled the minstrel,
thumbing a blues of lonely mailmen in blue shorts
carrying love letters up and down the streets
of Bohemian suburbs nostalgic for Woodstock
and Watergate's clarity, that manifesto of revolution
swirling in the veins like an altered states of America,
but ending, surreally, in baby-boomer bands
of gray-haired men and women astride
tiny scooters revving at the stop sign
like a Harley-biker retirement club.
It doesn't get any sadder than this, he says,
lifting his sake glass for another round.

While the monk, eyeing his spent cup,
whistles that same tune all the way home
—half empty half full—
as though desire were a failed revolution
still thundering in the mouth as the last
great song on the face of the earth.

How To Know God

Pull up a chair and offer Her a beer,
no come-ons, everyone's always wanting something.
Just sit and be silent awhile. Good talk comes slow.
Ask how long it's been since someone
patted Her on the back, or even knew
She's generally a Woman. Offer a few
encouraging words, that it's tough being
in charge of such a raucous brood as humanity.
Don't speak too quickly about your own
petty needs and desires, that will come later,
and She'll be happy to listen, then, to each one.
Order a second round, pay for them both;
it's all Her money anyway, but She won't mind—
that's what She made it for. Describe what it's like
where you live, how things shake down here
on the front lines, the advantages and disadvantages
of the cosmic trickle-down effect, how bad things
sometimes happen to good people and vice-versa,
but how it's all still really beautiful and pretty amazing
that it works out as often as it does. She might be
impressed at your poise and general goodwill,
even think language wasn't such a bad invention after all,
what with the weird come-ons and prayers for bizarre things
She entertains every day. Rising from the corner chair,
She may even give you Her number, but don't come right out
and ask—see if you're chosen. It could be the beginning
of a meaningful relationship, both of you on the look-out
for something that will last past the honeymoon's glow
into the long stretch of unknown road ahead.

Why I Love Fundamentalists

I was playing basketball at the corner hoop
in Madison, Indiana, stroking the ball
like it was the grace of god on asphalt
in the parking lot of the Nazarene Church

when he cornered me, the preacher
guarding my escape till he could find
out who I was

just visiting my father-in-law
down the street

and his face lit up like Christmas
wanting to know if I *knew* the Lord
or was I lost, so I faked left

my father was a Nazarene preacher,
I've got several going back
generations on my mother's side.

He warmed to the task of finding out
if I was *walking* with the Lord now,
so I started dribbling fast but couldn't
escape the fact that at that moment

I was the center of his whole world,
he felt my life for all eternity
hung in the balance of his broad hands

and that my next decision would be
the most important one I'd ever make.

This is a rare experience in life, to be
so fully in focus, someone waiting
on your next act with each breath

and I basked in it—
but didn't want to lead him on unduly,
so took a shot from beyond the three-point arc

swish

and grinned, saying

don't know if I'm exactly walking
with the Lord, but he's sure running
fast trying to guard me.

The preacher smiled back as I jogged
down the street, uncertain
but thinking he had maybe
changed the life of one more soul forever

and for those few moments
when he and I were the only two people
who mattered on the face of the earth

he was right.

The Anonymity of Poets

If we had anything at all worth saying, wouldn't someone be listening? Wouldn't more than the few straggled round the beaten lectern, eyes closed, strands of words teasing the heart as Medusa's wild hair full of snakes—the venom of meaning, love's poisonous bite—wouldn't someone stand up, make a motion, a second, say *if not for this, we would have no heart!* How the world glistens as a deer gutted by the side of the road from collision with the careening speed of metal—the poet bending now over the still warm fur, dark pupils open, the transmission of something sacred, a last rite, the promise that this is not the end, that the wet nuzzle of nose, the thick clot of red, the quiet antler will live on, a reincarnation into word—this love for the world going on and on as lovers bantering into the night about the hard argument that if all was meant to be, why is it so hard to grasp, to say much beyond this *oooh & aagh* floating inarticulate out the throat as a soft orgasm or a death shudder when the earthquake that is your life rifles down your many faults and you split in two, trembling. If this was at all important, this speaking, somehow essential to the world going on and on as it does, wouldn't the stadiums fill at night, the therapists write new books claiming to have found their language at last, a grammar to shake politics down to the root, to infuse economists with the lyricism embedded in numbers, shake the ennui from advertisers' brain stems, wouldn't the army brass sing a new anthem, everyone pledge a new allegiance to what lies inside these syllables? Tell me, is it worth saying, is any of this worth saying—words flapping like fish in rarefied air, waiting to be thrown back into the dark waters from whence we come, though the world is hungry— and we, fishers of the deep, with only this thin thread, a hook, and one wriggling worm.

The Hindu Gods Are Laughing

An unlettered Dutch linen draper with his secret lenses
& magnifying glasses shocked the London Royal Society
with bread mold specimens, a bee's stinger, blood cells,
—his own saliva, excrement, semen—
none of which had been microscopically examined before.
Then, in a dab of pepper-water: *animalcules*, tiny protozoa.
A dead world suddenly teeming with life,
eight million beings in a single drop.

The Visitation

After his death, I shuffle through the contents of my father's study:
Japanese figurines on the wall, drawings for new pagodas & hexagons to
build. There, neatly lined in a row: five video tapes with our names labeled
in large black letters, waiting for this moment. I hand them out,

place one in the machine that brings him back to life. Watch him recall
the fleeting days of childhood: running through the orange groves of LA,
the treks to Venice beach, riding his bike, alone, everywhere—returning
home in the evening exhausted and aglow. For the first time, he is young
inside us: the red cheeks, faces burning wet.

After the Amputation

At ninety-five in the nursing home, Aunt Opal says
I don't know where my leg is, and my mother replies
someone's taking good care of it. Her dead husband,
forgotten. Her small house, not even a memory.
But the body knows when something is lost:
how the spirit, severed at birth, has trouble
staying in skin and bone.

Secret of the Universe

The watermelon waits in the refrigerator—
red, succulent flesh encased in green
tough alligator skin. I could crack it,
ravage its interior with wild hunger.
Instead, pull knife from wooden block,
slice one delicate line then another
into the wet heart till it opens, revealing
nothing that can be explained. Only tasted.

What Is Deep Is Not Beyond Reach

Maybe it was the dolphin in Jamaica,
swimming belly-up in the bay so I could
skim its silken skin. Or my friend's story

of three humpback whales circling
under her boat. There is another life
wet, alien, immense—

just beneath the mind, swimming
in the body. Wild, ordinary. Is it
love, or instinct that threatens

to capsize my careful boat,
grow dorsal fin,
swim.

The Spiritual Life of Cats

From my backyard swing,
I see gulls circling beyond the fence,
palm fronds whipping in wind like a kite,
the black squirrel chewing a brown nut
large as its own head. My cat Sara
sits with me, considering everything.

Gophers haunt the ground,
but Sara has abandoned stalking the unseen.
For now. Though I catch her near sunset
staring pensively at an empty hole, listening,
listening.

Obstinacy As a Spiritual Strategy

The immense Monterey Pine lies on its side,
fallen near the cliffs overlooking the Pacific.
Last decade's storm toppled it one night,
root and dirt base exposed seaward. But
the pine still grows—green as ever,
immense as ever.

It is not enough to be defeated.

Even with the vertical abandoned—
there is life on the axis, here:

the stubborn gnarl that binds,
the sky now seen from new vantage.

Sound of One Angel Clapping (Falling)

Every morning, I hear it—the crows
flap from tree to tree cawing their joyful lament.
I rise, arch my shoulders to ease tightened muscles
from night's lifeless repose—reach back to touch
the bony stubs where, once again, I dreamt wings grew.
Remorseless, I walk rather than fly into the day,
into a world I will one day give everything to.

Grace

In the dark of Esalen's bar—
wooden tables, black chairs, colored Christmas lights—
she says *There is more grace in the world than we can see,*
says her small boy will never speak,
devilish gene robbing him of voice, fingers—
but his shaman eyes appear in people's dreams,
speaking there what cannot be said here. One day,
a passing Buddhist monk stopped
at his baby carriage, asked to pay respects
to such a teacher. *There is more grace*

in this world than you can see echoes another
of her brother the psychedelic seeker, lost
chasing the Gordian knot of consciousness,
spiking his coffee with magic mushrooms
which she drank, unknowingly, during a visit.
Later, as she stopped her car on the ridge to view
phantasmagoric pine, undulating asphalt,
she glimpsed for a few hours the landscape
her brother cannot escape. Outside the bar,

down the hill in the warm sulfur baths,
a Brazilian healer prays over the tumors
in another friend's belly, the waves
beneath the cliffs sounding a kind of grace.
In this morning, she will come to us at breakfast
at this same wooden table, say
she wants more of this, the only life
she knows. This one,
where she is eating oatmeal
in small spoonfuls, in a black chair,
lips savoring dark sugar, sweet milk.

The Gift

Now that she is gone,
I peer at the small painted Mexican box
blue with yellow flowers, Mother Mary behind glass,
that my friend with cancer brought back
from a small village. Did they both
wonder what grew in their bellies,
a curse, a blessing,
the womb's extravagance?
Let's not pretend Mary knew, at first,
any more than my friend: a stirring
in the abdomen's soft muscle,
cells dividing, multiplying.
Who could understand what the archangel
meant, touching her there, saying
it was a gift. Chosen
to bring forth, then surrender
this one perfect life.

The Only Truth I Know

I open the door to the outhouse in the Sierras,
find a Jehovah's Witness *Watchtower* perched on wooden beam.
With the forest in front of me, I sit, turn the pages,
read of God's plan, the end times, remember
that sense of mission, of surety, as a boy
when all I needed to know was in that one black book.
It is seductive, here in the wilderness, to believe in revelation.
The lake speaks to me at night, the granite murmurs,
the fire cracks and whistles its prophecies.
But the young ranger, who speaks reverently
of the hungry bear roaming these woods,
says it had to be put down. It wasn't afraid
enough of humans. I am afraid,

which is why I love the woods. For a moment
forgetting politicians who believe in Armageddon,
the ideologues who are happy to oblige, trigger-happy cowboys
of every ilk staring towards the horizon, revelation
gleaming in their eyes, fingering destiny. Absolute surety.
It is a feeling I would give almost anything

to regain. Place the pamphlet, instead, back on its perch,
hike back to the lake's edge, remove my clothes,
stand naked to the only truth I know.
Jump into water so cold, so clear.

Endless Forms Most Beautiful

> — Quote from Darwin

The stunning double helix of DNA
embodies the sum of our genes in each cell,
humans with roughly the same number
as mice, tiny worms only somewhat less.
All possibilities exist in each cell—
the flippers of whales,
the wings of bats—
why then do we become
one thing, and not another?
What spirit summons,
what enzyme triggers
two eyes or a thousand,
warm blood or cold?
With no single gene for an eye,
a limb, a language, we are all
variations of a single love,
a kind of obsession—the way
a fertilized egg knows to become
a whale, a cow, a child
with unrelenting epochal passion.
Deep in the eye of my father,
the smooth skin of my mother,
some desire of Adam remains,
the scent of Eve, incubated
in me by an unrelenting god,
desire engorged, this swooning
need to take shape—a dream
of double-helixed divinity—
becoming the unfathomable thing I am,
this one and only
of endless forms most beautiful.

The Way God Laughs

The blackened duck with long neck
sits on the plate of the Frenchman.
He fingers his long handlebar mustache,
looks mischievously over at us, winks—
then laughs as his wife poses
behind the plate of duck for a picture.
The young Balinese waitress
cuts the duck's neck,
hands it to the Frenchman,
who winks again and chases the girl
back to the kitchen with the black head.
Here, laughter and death mix.
The joy of the Frenchman,
the duck's delicious body,
the dark earth, inscrutable,
waiting.

Trust

The green plastic plants
I placed high in wicker baskets
hang from the ceiling in order
to remain unchanging, beautiful.
Somehow, they still lose their leaves,
exposing plastic stubs covered with dust.
My every attempt to bolster against decay
defeated. I throw them in the blue recycle bin,
buy real ferns, the kind I can trust
not to promise eternity.

My Sometime Spiritual Life

God is like oyster with lemon, an acquired taste;
a clarity, like coffee at midnight, like diesel spilled

across concrete floor to cut the oil of your broken engine
lying in pieces from long nights of tinkering. His

knuckles are implacable, kneading the body's knots,
bruising the heart's membrane. There is an aesthetic

to this loving. A violin in wooden box, cushioned
in velvet, played on afternoons while friends savor

sliced peaches. Often, it is more like the body of a dog
you have loved for years laid finally in the ground.

God is a voyeur looking for a life, a hostage of human
narrative, a used book thumbed endlessly.

My skull is sore from this trance I'm in, listening
to His studied seduction, like a fool on a blind date

scared this might be true love. Revelations like plumes
of bar-room smoke drift in my eyes. Eyelashes charred

from peering too close at such opaque fire. But I am
finding my swagger. I am cursing up a psalm.

Let the angels blanch.

I am kissing this damned world!

The Art of Suffering

He felt God the same way arthritic monks felt rain coming in their joints.
He felt only the hint of him.
—Sue Monk Kidd

Wag More, Bark Less...
–Bumper Sticker

A layman will no doubt find it hard to understand
how pathological disorders of the body and mind can be
eliminated by "mere" words.
He will feel that he is being asked to believe in magic.
And he will not be so very wrong.
—Sigmund Freud

The First Mark of Existence

Peter and I hike under gray skies
through a forest bent on overtaking the old road.
Red Manzanita has grown to a thick impenetrable maze.
Amid pine, cedar and oak, hundreds of smaller wizened trees
turn black from lack of light as they clamor for sun
beneath the wide branches of elders.

But we are happy, speaking of Buddhism
as we veer up the hillside where a path still lies
if you can find it, muse on *anicca*, the Pali word
for *impermanence*, the first Mark of Existence
in Buddhist thought, and who can argue—
the rain bursting sudden, soaking the clay ranger road,
knocking small branches from pines onto our heads.

This craving for permanence, Buddha said,
is the root of suffering in a world where change
is the only constant. I tell Peter of my sadness
watching mother valiantly age while her body fails,
and the small hexagon cabin she lives in
fades into the forest like mist. His eyes
reflect mine as it stops raining.

Beneath our feet, hundreds of tiny trees
arch again from clay towards light.

A Buddhist Riddle: To Lose the Self

Clive has the rarest amnesia ever recorded. A simple virus—cause of the common cold-sore—traveled to his brain, wiping out his memory. Now, every conscious moment is like waking for the first time, just seven seconds long. Though he plays piano still—music part of body-memory, like walking or riding a bike. Playing each note, he seems like any other man, only more so. When the score ends, he stops, becomes lost in the moment again. What monks spend a lifetime seeking, Clive cannot escape. Who is it, then, that becomes enlightened?

Original Desire

Inside the bottle of clear wine from Vietnam, two snakes are wound round each other in an infinity sign. The green-mamba cobra, head fanned and arched toward the bottle's spout, is encircled by a long, thin snake biting the cobra's neck. This *Snake Wine: for Rheumatism, Lumbago, Sweat of Limbs* is shared between friends, sold by corner shamans. After all, it was the snake that seduced—shedding worn skin, emerging golden. Sip by sip, I inoculate my bottomless desire.

A Song of Death & Life During Christmas

Dining at Otto's on Main St. in Covington,
across the Ohio River from Cincinnati's lights,
my wife, her brother and I talk all evening of death.
Not in a macabre way, nor morose, but intimate
sipping a Shiraz, enjoying blackened chicken,
grilled tilapia, scallops savored in dim light, a bit of jazz.
Our conversation lingers on a father in Indiana
sitting in his lounger petting a small dog, waiting;
his wife beside him in her own chair, nursing broken ribs
from her latest fall with white wine and murder shows,
waiting. In California, my mother is in a chair
with her dog saved from the pound,
watching videos about crop circles and dolphins,
psychics and news from the *other side*, waiting.
All of this swirls inside us, sitting in Otto's
waiting for the check, not anxious to leave
because it is so warm inside, and this conversation,
so overdue, sits in our throats ruby as wine,
secreting from us the way we'd chose to go,
pondering how we even arrived at this exact moment.
Our parents' meeting so dependent on chance:
an English bride for a young Kentucky boy—
and a California couple courting in church
near the orange groves of Los Angeles.
One look leading to another, a gift of rings,
the flush of sex, the making of a life—
birthing the children who sit now round this languid table.
Sipping our last bit of Shiraz, we walk into the cold night
listen to carolers, linger inside each note.
We are in no hurry for the sonorous end to come.

Such Brilliant Light

My wife visits the Creation Museum in Kentucky
with her brother, the agnostic, and her sister
an evangelical Catholic. They
enter the museum's lavish new grounds
greeted by beaming young guides
who entreat visitors to keep an open mind—
that science has been wrong in the past,
that the earth could, truly, have been made
in six days, the dinosaurs in the ark,
Cain mating with his sister, not a poisonous
mushroom or snake in sight. Scene after scene
in the spanking-new halls intone that the universe
is not a soulless clock ticking in evolutionary tintinnabulation,
but the breath of God rising from the mists
of darkness, called forth into a light so bright
we needed only have rested in creation's perfection
rather than biting that seductive apple.

Home again, my wife unravels this story aghast,
looks into my eyes to gauge response. I arch
my brow, smile, find myself saying we are indeed
the breath of God rising in the darkness,
that one divine day seems to last a millennium,
that the ticking clock of the world *is* filled with soul,
a metronome of evolutionary wildness
springing forth from God's laughter
and—the divine inside joke—that we split
all things into pairs: science and faith,
belief and reason all carried in the body's ark.

My wife laughs, expects nothing less from me,
files the visit away as yet another mystery
that we—half ape, half angel—
will mull into eternity's *tick-tock, tick-tock.*
Each morning contemplating
the apple,
its smooth skin of mystery,
the next delicious bite.

The Devil's Blues

On the top floor of the Belle of Cincinnati riverboat,
an autistic Chinese boy plays with a yellow rope,
lofts it over the side, watches it flutter into the Ohio River.
Banjo music lilts the heart as huge rear paddles
slowly propel us upriver, a black pirate flag
flapping in the wind. It was here southern slaves
crossed over to the north, braving currents, ice,
shotguns. Now, the banjo player sings
Keep on the sunny side, always on the sunny side of life...
while a small plump girl in pink twirls round a pole
with a handful of thick pretzels in hand. It is
the kind of day when all complaints, all laments
fall away—where even the ugly meanness of life
is a kind of dark praise.

No Small Feat

Along the Ganges river, Hindu sages summon
the extraordinary from within: a woman living buried
in an airless pit for three days; an old man whose arm,
now withered, has been raised overhead since he was a boy;
the wandering *saddhus* who roll their penises round a pole,
invite strangers to stand on it. And I,

who must do no less, crawl inside my body each morning,
tenderly fill each limb, each weary bone—
incarnate again into the ordinary day.

Origin Stories

Sitting in the café, the waitress brings a tray of tiny paper shot glasses filled with Komodo Dragon dark coffee, offers bite size brownies, then the shot to bring out the *citrus, floral essence* of the bitter brew. And it *is* heaven—not cloud and angel and light—but a taste in the palate, then down the tongue, of darkness so delicious, so heavy, I know why Satan—the brightest of archangels—fell *here*.

Love Affair

Three men stand on the curved cliffs overlooking a nude beach,
each positioned far from the other, but staring nonchalantly
down, then out to sea, then back again. The beach
is tucked away from sight, but can be found
if one knows where to look. I walk by, pause—
expect to see sun-bathing women worshipped
by the three strangers. Instead, there is only the sea.
The four of us in love, now,
with the same woman.

Sacred Texture

Rain on the roof, bamboo flute—the masseuse presses her palm, then thumb, deep beneath shoulder, finds the knot, the pain. *Touch* is the way God kisses this tender bruise of body—as though God were blind, my skin the Braille by which I am read.

The Farther Lights

A man sits by the campfire contemplating regrets,
looking to the stars for divine order.
Lake Eleanor is calm under the half moon.
She is calm, like a woman who knows
how thoroughly she is loved, though
only half her dreams are illumined.
The other half dark.
Though the thin, gray outline
of its concave shape is clearly seen
against the greater darkness.

Like a man, there is also a side
of the moon facing away, never seen.
Always in darkness.
Always facing the farther lights,
those immense hydrogen engines
illuminating desire's edge.

But tonight, both moon and lake are calm,
knowing they are loved. And the man
is calm in the steady pulse of his body.
The fire embering a handful of regrets
into ash.

Years in the Making

Old windows lie cracked, discarded
between garage and decayed fence,
falling to the ground this winter's rain
after years of steady standing. I wade in,
untangle thorny blackberry vines
from rusted nails, buried brick,
the mud of what has been ignored.
Leather gloves protect each hand
as pruning shears clip vines down
to the ground; later, a little poison
for each root, the only protection
from such uncanny, wild growth.
How the years sway, the vigor of rain,
holy marriage of mulch and sprig,
the eager entropy of life once set
in motion, so impossible
to stem. Who is to say
what may grow, where, for how long?
On this small plot of ground,
I do—wielding shovel, clipper, rake.
But inside

this cranium, cracked window
of soul, all the fence boards have fallen,
thorn and nail tear at heart bereft of cover,
everything a tangle of vine, broken brick,
glass shards slivering their small, sad songs
along each fingerprint. Here,
there is no master, only the making
of callous, the mending of wounds,
the shoveling—one wheelbarrow
at a time carrying the detritus
of what it means to be *human*

towards the compost pile. Years
in the making,

I spread the mulch of me around,
work into ground what has decomposed,
feel underneath to where my own slow poison
has yet to kill the root of me. How fortunate
some part knows better, returns again
with a clamor, sweet juice dark as blackberry
running down my cheek.

A Fortune-Teller Told Me

Tizian Terzani, an Italian-born journalist, lived in Asia
reporting for the German newsmagazine *Der Spiegel.*
Warned by a Hong Kong fortune-teller not to fly one year,
he traveled by foot, boat, bus, train—doubting
each step of the way. Of course, never really *believing*
the prediction—he was a journalist. Only coincidence
could explain the crash of the U.N. helicopter over Cambodia,
the one he would have been on. The pathos of Asia
for soothsayers & shamans only explained their backwardness.
But many of us have a person we don't talk much about—
the crazy aunt who reads Tarot, the gypsy palm-reader
from Berkeley, the acupuncturist who studies your feet,
your elbows. In my family, it was a friend named Sandy—
housewife with a cigarette, living in a non-descript track-home
stuck like an afterthought along Highway 99.
No crystal ball, no purple robe—just your watch in her hand,
a necklace, something of you. Closing her eyes, she'd begin
speaking—and there you were, as though Hemingway
was describing your life, or Kerouac. Even the police
hired her to find missing persons, solve murders.

The world speaks in many ways—
not always linear as a lawyer. Sometimes heavenly spheres
will whisper, numbers appear random, then lure you
with sudden design. There is a conversation going on
between everything—this should come as no surprise:
the nuclei of ants, the testosterone of generals, the dreams
of Malaysian girls asleep in the brothel. Everything is speaking:
even the soft pulp of *future*, the hard rind of *past*
splitting open like a watermelon. The brain tastes
what it wants to know, curls the tongue round
what it doesn't—spitting each black seed
on the ground with relish.

In the beginning

it must have been like this:
a small boy sitting on the floor, hunched over
his new electric football set unwrapped in all its glory,
attention fused, timeless, as one miniature football player
after another is placed halfway between two opposite goals.
The polarities inherent in any game, squaring off in pairs,
a jolt of electricity every few seconds vibrating the board,
the subtle dynamics of each player's plastic feet
a kind of evolutionary determinism: which one
will be stronger, faster, move straight ahead or curve
endlessly in circles. The boy,

a god, lingering over the nuances of combination:
which ones, together, make the best team, the worst,
or perfectly paired as equal adversaries in the yin & yang
of struggle, the eloquent teamwork, the kaleidoscope
of competition more addictive than its opposite:
this dull calm of knowing that the vast spaces of suburbia
stretch like endless dark matter in a vacuum with no boundary—
the universe, the young child delighting
in the joyous clash of every unknown: *what will happen next?*
The possibility of creation its own balm,
galactic enterprise in the personal,

this *to be or not to be* haunting the vacant seconds
ticking in the catacombs of DNA,
each synapse a nerve-bridge between spirit & matter,
the world a hologram, the board, the boy, the plastic limbs
with kneepad & cleat, the helmeted heads, the contrary goals
at either end of this spectrum of progress or regression,
this whole damn thing (blessed beyond mere joy)
the reason

that each morning a sun rises in the vastness,
coloring the black sky purple, then orange, finally blue.
The boy lazes from his bed, still in pajamas,
and it's Sunday, and today just like yesterday,
just like any other eon, anything could happen.
Anything.

Sizing Up the World

There's nothing here of interest to me
said the fat boy with glasses, head buried in yet another book
when I asked why he didn't pay more attention
to what was going on. I couldn't blame him,
straddled as I was, too, between worlds—
the interior mind endless as a multi-verse,
the exterior world boring as a parking lot
but stubbornly real. Now the other boys
could make a parking lot infinitely interesting
with their pickup trucks and speed demon cars
parked and purring while the girls with short skirts
sidled up. But beyond this, it was just garbage-can alleys
& bowling alleys where boys grew to be men,
balls in the gutter, throwing their lives away.
It's tough when you reach your pinnacle at eighteen,
slide down the backside as though there was really
someplace to go, but there's not—
prom king & queen surveying the small town they'd inherit,
eyes fading into the dusky blur of a world too small
for dream.

Except for the nerd with glasses, imagination
rolling in his skull, rollicking in his cranium
through telescope and microscope,
universes careening off the page with a big-bang.
He was a prophet of sorts, sacred books
of science fiction and fantasy opening
the dark side of moon, the rage of demon-dragons,
the light that would not be put out—

even as the football jocks passed us in the hallway,
jostle and insult a daily gauntlet.
As though the darkness had taken sneering shape
in high school corridor and locker room hell.
It was then I decided
heroism was no fantasy, that this planet
was stranger than most and I would need to keep my wits,
would need to become a wizard of sorts—
the world an unpredictable story, and I,
bespectacled devourer of universes,
holding a burning staff in my sweaty,
trembling hand.

Golden Dragon

My young son talks all evening about past lives,
as though he could not be contained in eight meager years.
Uncle Steven had visited, talking with Gabriel
about reincarnation while doing odd jobs around the house.
Now, the stories come—how he remembers being a monkey,
a man who invented pencils, the way in which he died
each time. Most of all, he remembers being a Chinese warrior
poised over an enemy when an arrow hit his forehead,
sword swinging into his opponent as they fell.
He says dying isn't so bad after all—

you feel pain at first, but then you don't.
He says this with such conviction that I believe every word.
Twirling about the room, he puts on a yellow Chinese hat
made of silk, golden dragons circling the small red tassel
on top, a long braid attached. The one he picked out
in San Francisco's China Town, the one present he must have.
Perhaps he was picking up where he left off,
braiding the threads of his life together. And I think:

I will love you in any guise, my young dragon—
see how he beats the air with his arms, already lifting away
into the only life I can bear losing him to.

Leaning Towards the Southern Hemisphere

Samara, Costa Rica

Veranda, hammock—refuge from what I'd become.
Small red frogs with immense toes sit silent
in trees nearby, poisonous, bearing witness.

Forgetting myself, I worship every cocoanut husk,
green parrot, afternoon rain. Even mosquitoes
sound like singing, feel like tiny bruised kisses.
All insolence drains from my body,
reverence the only tongue I know.

There is something here: milk inside the husk.
Beneath the ground, a single bean germinates.

Inside the bean, a mountain grows:
this doppelganger life—a shadow,
a savior.

A Buddhist in Tuscany

Last night, slices of prosciutto,
wheat crackers and cheese, red wine.
The quiet hills, the wind. This morning,
a bed in a room with two windows,
a washing bowl of well water, a white towel,
a desk. With a few simple things,
I could make a life—wash away envy,
dab this wounded craving with white cloth,
watch it turn blood red, color of the vineyard,
color of what burns in my veins, this delicious
drunken ruby need.

The Taste of Light

Last night, on a balcony just north of Venice,
I could almost believe the world was becoming
light. Four glasses, a decanter, Italian wine—
dinner with our former nanny Jen, her new husband Andrea.
They met in Germany speaking Spanish together
over beer steins, settling here in Jesolo, Italy,
speaking with us now in a mix of Italian, English.
Jen pregnant, Andrea a master chef yearning for America,
to start a restaurant, raise a family. They are so young,
have little idea of the dark underbelly of dream.
But tonight, the warmth of the night,
the Italian hospitality, the food, the wine,
the balcony pointing towards a Venice you can't see
but know is there—I can almost believe the world,
its inventive mix of pigment and language,
this volatile fermenting of dream and despair,
the aged flavor of my wife's eyes,
the nip of decades, exuberant, mournful, pleasing.
I can almost taste in the bottom of my glass
this hidden light emanating from our bodies.
How we are sipped, savored, sung by darkness
for our hint of aural radiance caught
between sad lip and ecstatic tongue.

Love at The Gun Runner

At the edge of town in Merced, California, sits a pale building whose sign says, "The Gun Runner". A shooting range and retail outlet for rifles, pistols, and any kind of bullet you might need, it is owned and operated by Sandy, a friend of my family's and the only true psychic I know. Her husband, Gary, whom I've never met, helps her run the place. I haven't seen Sandy for years, not since my father died and she came to the funeral to tell my mother, my siblings, and me what Dad wanted her to communicate: that he had passed over and was filled with love for us and awe at life's immensity and regret over whatever hurt his depression might have caused everyone. We trusted Sandy and always welcomed her glimpses into the "other side".

Shortly after that, Sandy stopped giving psychic readings. Too many people asked the same questions: *Will I find love? Is my spouse cheating? Am I going to win the lottery?* Then there were those who were looking for some purpose or meaning in life, but they all wanted her to give them the Answer. Sandy was more interested in helping people find their own answers within. So she retired and opened a gun shop with Gary.

For years my mother has been saying I should stop by the Gun Runner sometime to say hello to Sandy. So I pull into the shop's parking lot as dusk descends. The lights are on inside, and I venture through the double glass doors, still wearing my shirt and tie from a state mental-health meeting in Sacramento. I'm nervous and unfamiliar with how to behave in a gun store, and the bearded man behind the front counter eyes me suspiciously. Then I spy Sandy behind the cash register in back. She grins and acts surprised to see me. (You never know with psychics.) We embrace and look each other over and catch up on our lives: the big dreams we have, the small ways in which we live them out. I tell her about the tragedy of a relative's drug addiction. She tells me about the suicide of a stranger on the shooting range and the time a stray bullet ricocheted up a ventilation shaft and went through a wall Sandy had been standing next to seconds before. (Her intuition had told her to move just then.) And she describes her new joy: a small group that gathers on Wednesdays at her home to discuss their psychological and spiritual development. In this life, she says, it all boils down to love.

The bearded man who eyed me as I entered the store saunters over and puts his arm around Sandy. "This is Gary," Sandy says, and he and I shake hands before he's called away to help a customer who has a question about bullets. Sandy tells me Gary is the most loving soul she knows. Each morning before they open the gun shop, they hold hands and pray to provide a small oasis of light for every customer who comes through their doors. Sandy leans close to me and whispers, "Gary looks right at each person who walks in and silently says to them: *I love you.*" What more could you ask for in this world?

The Art of Suffering

In the Japanese section of the Metropolitan Art Museum,
I walk amid serene Buddhas and silk screens.
Two security guards speak of their pains—
torn rotator cuff, sore back, the injury claims.
Glancing at the ancient bodhisattvas all around,
I'm sure I detect smiles so subtle the Mona Lisa
would appear to be laughing out loud.

A Crack Between Two Worlds: Poetry and the Art of Suffering

A Talk by Dane Cervine
for the Ina Coolbrith Circle Poetry Awards Banquet
November 1, 2008 in Orinda, California

The poet, and local laureate Connie Post, heard me read in the Century House series last February, intrigued by my background as a therapist, a Buddhist practitioner, and a poet. After, we mused on the role of human suffering, psychology, and its relationship to poetry, as well as poetry and its possible healing affects on the wounded mind. I am thankful for the opportunity to consider these questions, and since we are poets, to begin with a poem entitled 'A Crack Between Two Worlds' from my book *The Jeweled Net of Indra:*

A Crack Between Two Worlds

I remember Paul, his diagnosis: schizophrenia—and who could argue.

Sitting across from me on the edge of his chair, eyes like Jupiter moons,

alive with the secret he kept but shared with me now:

that the solar system was his, as far as Saturn's rings,

maybe even beyond. Then there was me: world shrunken

to my perimeter of body, the narrow passage of mind,

the dull glare of reality. When it comes to this machine of brain,

the *true* or *false* litmus of belief, there is only one test here: sanity,

or its opposite. What poet could pass such exam without cheating,

what artist answer with any confidence? There is a crack in the world,

full of names—calling us to peer in, pull out our own secret

from the bowels of earth. A radio dial

spans a wide band of frequency, but even this is too narrow a gauge.

Beyond what we can hear, see, lies the farther spectrum

of infrared light, rays of gamma, pitch of sound so high as to drive

a dog crazy—while we look about blankly, hear nothing. It is good

to be careful. The closer you listen, you risk losing—an ear, a career,
a life. But what is horizontal in us begs the vertical, to meet here
in the body as a cross, to spread arms and legs wide saying
touch the holes in my hands, the holes in my feet,
feel the wound in my side. Even our gods

are over the edge. So this is what we face: everyday,
to be a ladder into the crevice, to pull ourselves out again,
whichever side we stand upon, to be a bridge for the other,
a thread for the wounds between.

There are a range of very legitimate, and contrary, perspectives on this topic of poetry and suffering: do writers and artists suffer more acutely, and more often, than other folks? Is it to some extent a requirement for creative genius? If we suffered less, would our art have less depth, be less compelling? Is there hope for healing in poetry itself? On the one hand, we have:

• Billy Collins, former U.S. poet laureate, who feels that no suffering is needed per se for his poems to emerge. That they emerge from the quiet, curious contemplation illustrated in his poems, as he wanders his house musing on jazz, butterflies, and Zen temple bells.

• William Carlos Williams, who wrote poems on the back of envelopes and prescription pads while he went about his work as a doctor.

• Wallace Stevens, a lawyer his entire life who became vice-president of the Hartford Accident and Indemnity Company, as well as a nationally known poet. He believed pursuing the two in combination gave his life character.

So at least the outward appearance of the intense suffering experienced by some writers is not a requirement for the calling—though it is always difficult to weigh private pain shielded from public view. Still, there may be some truth to the perception that writers and artists suffer more than others. The field of psychology is beginning to shed some light on this topic.

In *The Awakenings Review*, a poetry journal from the University of Chicago Center for Psychiatric Rehabilitation, editor Robert Lundin reviews the prevalence of mental illness among poets, including depression, mania, and psychosis. He cites several studies:

• Arnold Ludwig from the University of Kentucky wrote *The Price of Greatness: Resolving the Creativity and Madness Controversy*. He reviewed the New York Times book section over a thirty year period, picked biographies of the famous and great, analyzed them for incidence of depression, mania, and psychosis. A staggering 18% of the poets he studied had committed suicide. Writers evidenced 2 to 3 times the average rate of psychosis, suicide attempts, mood disorders, and substance abuse. The rate of forced hospitalization was 6 to 7 times that of non-artistic groups studied.

• Celebrated John Hopkins psychologist Kay Redfield Jamison wrote *Touched with Fire: Manic-Depressive Illness and the Artistic Temperament*. In related work, she studied the proclivity of British and Irish poets of the 18th century to "madness". More than half of the 36 poets she reviewed demonstrated evidence of a mood disorder. The rate of commitment to asylums was twenty times that of the non-literary population.

• Nancy Andreason of the University of Iowa studied contemporary writers in the Iowa Writer's Workshop. Of the 30 she studied, 80% reported some mood or substance abuse problem, compared to 30% for a control group of writers.

These figures far exceed the Surgeon General's national prevalence rates for mental/emotional disorders, which affect approximately 20% of the population and trail only heart disease as the most prevalent national health concerns. Those involved by necessity or choice with creative pursuits do seem to lead the pack.

So what are we to advise poets, ourselves, about the wild terrain of the unruly mind? Here's another poem, based on the experience of a woman I know who wrestles with bipolar disorder. The title alludes to the Buddhist notion that with endless heavens above, and endless hells below (whether mental or mythical), it is only in this "middle world" one can truly awaken:

The Middle World Where We Live

At the conference, she sat on stage telling her story: about the onset of mania so sweet God could be felt, intimate—the world finally making sense. How she shed her clothes on the shore, her jewelry in the sea—swimming naked towards a sense of arrival, some greater thing awaiting her in the waves beyond. And when the police helicopters circled,

urging her back to shore, how she went, dutifully, more naked than before—gold & diamonds lost under wave. The days in the psych-ward, the thick-tongued medication rooting her in body & bone. Then, walking out again into the soberness of never arriving—the clarity of doubt, the fickle dance of meaning—the world again a mix of heaven, and its absence.

So on the one hand we have the Billy Collins, Wallace Stevens, and William Carlos Williams of the world. On the other, the Byrons, Lowells, Sextons, Berryman and Plaths of the world—where debilitating depression, mania, and sometimes suicide seem to be the price of creative genius. Perhaps living in this "middle world" is not possible for some artists and writers, or the price—the loss of one's *muse* or *genius*—too steep. Yet the allure of finding some measure of health, of sanity, even while listening to this muse, also lies at the center of the human.

In yet another vein, we have the poetry of ecstasy, the illuminating work of Rumi, Kabir, Hafiz, Mirabai, a deep strain of mystical poetry that seems to emanate from a profound union with God and an all-encompassing embrace of the world. What are we to make of this? Are poets also more likely to experience ecstasy, as well as suffering? Can suffering be somehow transmuted through the mysticism of poetry?

The existentialist and psychologist, as well as the Buddhist, would say that *suffering* is a common, universal human experience shared by all. In fact, the Buddhists identify the common reality of suffering as the First Noble Truth—though we often avoid facing it squarely.

From this beginning point of shared suffering, the ecstatic poetry of Sufi and Hindu poets represent a breakthrough in the tremendous paradoxical struggles inherent in human life—but often only after a "dark night of the soul". These breakthroughs do not come easy, and are often interrupted by periods of great despair when the Beloved or the Guest does not appear. At their best, they reflect an integration of dark and light, of yin and yang, an alchemical smelting of suffering till, finally, healing occurs, and ecstasy appears.

Given this existential/Buddhist view of *suffering* as ever-present and the ground of our human experience, how do poets like Billy Collins give expression to such depths and subtleties without apparent intense personal suffering?

In the language of psychology, there are two main approaches to therapy that may offer a parallel to poetry: uncovering techniques, and structuring techniques. In therapy, depending on the nature of the individual and the type of dis-ease, uncovering techniques take suffering apart bit by bit (witnessing) till it disappears; structuring techniques, on the other hand, focus on "the good," utilizing cognitive-behavioral approaches that structure perception to ride through the psycho-physical waves which threaten to sink one's small boat.

Perhaps poets fall along a similar continuum in their approach to writing, some in the camp of tearing apart their experience with the sword of the Word while battling dark forces, while others concentrate more on the sound of life's "hum," or the "Om" it makes when we let in its beauty—transcending suffering in the process. But suffering in the existential, psychological, or Buddhist sense must be present in some measure for poetry to avoid a mere Pollyanna, sentimentality that is comforting, but shallow. To let the Spanish notion of *duende* in, the dark pathos that brings depth and flavor to life. My suspicion is that all good poets mine the depth and breadth of human life through some level of contact with suffering, whether the path is direct or indirect, subtle or obvious.

Though on the surface I am not victimized by clinical bouts of depression or other dis-eases, as a therapist I recognize in myself the archetype of the shaman as "wounded healer," and that my poetry emerges in part from a history of my father's depression; on my mother's side, a legacy of eldest sons who were "eccentric," flirting with mental illness; and of course my own existential nature, capable of both ecstasy and despair in all things human.

So, a wry poem now about the *art of suffering*, since it is perhaps the way that we suffer, or write, that gives life its texture:

The Art of Suffering

In the Japanese section of the Metropolitan Art Museum, I walk amid serene Buddhas and silk screens. Two security guards speak of their pains—torn rotator cuff, sore back, the injury claims. Glancing at the ancient bodhisattvas all around, I'm sure I detect smiles so subtle the Mona Lisa would appear to be laughing out loud.

So for those of us who do suffer more obviously, what can poetry do? Does it truly offer help, healing, the possibility of integration of our contrary parts?

I think the healing effects of poetry are as profound as the literary genius sprung from suffering. Most have heard, or felt, the experience of "if not for this poem, I'm not sure I would have made it". Or, "because of this poem, my life will never be the same". In this way, poetry matters profoundly, and is healing. Poetry has proved helpful in my work as director of Santa Cruz County's child, youth and family programs. Every year I include client poetry in our program evaluation reports, often written by youth in juvenile hall through classes taught by Dennis Morton (one of the co-founders of Poetry Santa Cruz). Often this work is heartbreaking for the reader, and healing for the poet. Increasingly, Hip Hop spoken-word CD's and performances by youth are occurring at mental health conferences as both artistic and healing endeavors. In Santa Cruz, the Mental Health Client Action Network helps produce poetry and artwork by clients wrestling with serious mental and emotional illnesses, finding both just as necessary as medication and therapy for healing.

But it is not just in the field of Mental Health that poetry can be healing. For every poet, every reader of poetry, the written word itself can be a transmission of healing. Dr. Jeffrey Kripal, Chair of the Department of Religious Studies at Rice University, writes about a model of writing, reading and understanding:

> *...that is deeply hermeneutical—a model that recognizes how a truly profound engagement with a text can alter both the received meaning of the text, and one's own meaning and being...(that) is also physiologically true in regards to the "subtle body" of the brain's neural pathways...reading is an embodied practice that literally changes some of the body's most subtle processes...the act of reading, far from being a mechanical, disembodied exercise of vocabulary and grammar, is in fact an immeasurably complex psycho-physical event in which two horizons of meaning (the reader and the read) are "fused" and transfigured in a mysterious process that we do not, and perhaps cannot ever, fully understand...*

> *Reading/writing is a hermeneutical mysticism, an initiatory transmission, an altered state of consciousness.*

It is this deep listening that ultimately allows us to go on, in the face of a world—and an inner life—that can literally assault our neural pathways with both wonder and terror. Here's a poem I wrote about two scientists

who, by example, make me feel less self-conscious about the lengths to
which we must sometimes go to listen this deeply, and bear what is heard:

Thinking

Isaac Newton, upon swinging his feet out of bed in the morning,
would sit for hours immobilized by the sudden rush of thoughts
to his head. I don't feel so bad now, laboring as I do to cope.
With simple geometry, he determined the earth's weight.
In but an hour, I can find my breath, feel its pulse—

the weight of the world momentarily released—its own genius.

Then there was Lyell, a geologist, who when distracted by thought
would take up improbable positions on furniture: resting his head
on the seat of a chair while standing, or lying across two at once,
sinking so low that his buttocks would almost touch the floor.
To be so enamored with the world's layers, its momentous puzzle.

Would that I could stay in this position forever: the body arching
to bear the possible any way it can.

In the end, perhaps the shared mission of poetry and therapy can
be described in several ways. First, not to suffer unnecessarily, with
the guidance of whatever map we deem most useful—be it psychology,
meditation, or sheer stubborn will. Secondly, to recognize, as Dr Oliver
Saks says, "what a narrow ridge of normality we *all* inhabit, with the abysses
of mania and depression yawning to either side". And finally, as poets (in
the lines of my first poem):

*Every day, to be a ladder into the crevice, to pull ourselves out again—
whichever side we stand upon, to be a bridge for the other, a thread for the
wounds between.*

Praise for Dane Cervine's Poetry

Dane's acute observations bring a magnifying glass to the private and public Self, and his poems become our mirror. In this respect, Dane's work brings to mind Rilke's lines from the Duino Elegies: "All that we can achieve, here, is to recognize ourselves completely in what can be seen on earth."

—**Maggie Paul**, author of *Borrowed World*

∞

I keep Dane's poem "Sin" next to my computer to read each morning, and use the poem as the starting point for my workshop *Only This Failure to Praise: Poetry and Our Place in the World*. Dane Cervine tells us:

The worst part is failing to kiss the ground each morning.

Or the cold pot of resentment stirred and simmered

well into the evening. Everything else comes from this,

grows.

Using this poem as a guide, we explore our relationship to earth, to those closest to us, to abundance, to the material world, to death, and to spirituality.

— **Edwina Trentham**, editor of *Freshwater*

About the Author

Dane lives in Santa Cruz, California along the Monterey Bay coast, where he serves as Chief of Children's Mental Health for the county and works as a therapist.

Dane Cervine's book *The Jeweled Net of Indra* was published by Plain View Press in 2007. His poems have won or been finalists for awards from Adrienne Rich, Tony Hoagland, the Atlanta Review, and Caesura. His work appears in a diverse range of publications, including The SUN, the Hudson Review, anthologies, short film, animation, newspapers, and on-line.

Visit Dane Cervine's web site at **www.DaneCervine.typepad.com**.